CW00362650

CHINA & POTTERY

ANTIQUES POCKET GUIDE

CHINA & POTTERY

MARSHALL CAVENDISH

$\mathcal{P}$RICE GUIDE KEY

❶	Under £5	❻	£100 – £250
❷	£5 – £10	❼	£250 – £500
❸	£10 – £20	❽	£500 – £1000
❹	£20 – £50	❾	£1000 – £5000
❺	£50 – £100	❿	Over £5000

To help give you an idea of the value of a particular piece, each item is price-guided at the end of its caption. Look at the number in the circle at the end of the caption and check it against the price guide key on this page. This will show you the price range into which the pictured item falls.

Every care has been taken to ensure that the information given in this book is correct. However, the prices of antiques are subject to fluctuation. The publishers do not accept any liability for financial or other loss incurred through information contained in this book.

This edition published by Bookmart Ltd,
Desford Road, Enderby, Leicester LE9 5AD

Produced by Marshall Cavendish Books
(a division of Marshall Cavendish Partworks Ltd)
119 Wardour Street, London W1V 3TD

First printed in 1996
Copyright © Marshall Cavendish Limited 1996

ISBN 1 85435 867 7

Printed and bound in Singapore

CONTENTS

COLLECTING CHINA & POTTERY

FROM THE FINEST PORCELAIN TO THE SIMPLEST COTTAGE EARTHENWARE, CERAMICS HAVE ALWAYS BEEN ONE OF THE MOST POPULAR COLLECTABLES

Collecting ceramics can be done for many different reasons, but no matter why you collect, the more knowledge you have about the subject the more enjoyable it becomes. Indeed, some collectors find that the knowledge gained from research is as exciting as owning the antique china itself. This book concentrates on works from the major factories, and provides an ideal starting point for both absolute beginners, and more experienced treasure hunters. The price guides attached to each item give you the confidence to haggle with dealers right from the start.

If you're collecting for yourself, then buy what you like. Never buy simply as an investment. It is much better to splash out on something you will enjoy looking at, and get pleasure out of owning. Always go for quality, even if it does cost that little bit more. A good piece will hold its price and increase in value far better than a similar item from an inferior factory. In the same way, avoid damaged or restored pieces unless they fill that vital gap in your collection, and can be replaced at some later date.

Collecting antiques should not be just an exalted form of shopping. It is a fascinating pastime at which – like any other – you can always become more expert, learning by experience and finding out as much as you can. Like all forms of hunting it demands skill, tenacity and patience – even a bit of cunning. There may be long barren periods when nothing of any interest or value turns up, but every so often there will come the indescribable thrill of finding a real bargain.

Good Luck!

IDENTIFYING POTTERY

EARTHENWARE, ONE OF MANKIND'S OLDEST INVENTIONS, HAS BEEN GRADUALLY REFINED OVER THE LAST 500 YEARS TO BECOME A VERSATILE, PRACTICAL AND OFTEN HIGHLY DECORATIVE MATERIAL

E arthenware is a name given to anything made of moulded, baked clay. In its natural state, it is porous, and has to be glazed if anything liquid is to be kept in it. Types of earthenware are generally named for the different kinds of glazes, though in some, notably stoneware, a different manufacturing process is used.

Basic, unglazed earthenware, or biscuit, varies from pale buff, through brown to red, depending on the clay. Early earthenwares were sometimes decorated with slip, a watery solution of white or coloured clay. Sometimes this was trailed on, and sometimes, when it was used more thickly, it was moulded and applied to the pot.

The stoneware produced in the 17th century was made by heating the kilns to a higher temperature than that usually used for earthenware, thereby baking the clay to a stronger, non-porous material.

The next innovation was the introduction of creamware in the mid-18th century. Refined clay and calcined flint, baked at lower temperatures, produced an attractive, pale cream-coloured ware that was given a colourless glaze.

In 1800, stone china was patented in Staffordshire. Felspar was included in the clay to

▼ *This Mason's Ironstone ewer and basin of around 1820 is painted and gilded to mimic porcelain.* ❼

► *This creamware serving dish with impressed moulding and a pierced edge dates from the late 18th century.* ❼

create a heavy earthenware with a superficial resemblance to porcelain.

Throughout the 19th century, factories refined production to create even more colours and decorative finishes on earthenware. Mason's Ironstone china (*see page 40*) and Minton's majolica ware (*see page 56*) are both successful examples of this.

◄ *This 1868 majolica ware plate has the bright colours and basket weave design typical of such stoneware.* ❺

𝒟EALERS' TIPS

- Early creamware, from the 1760s and 1770s, can be distinguished by its thick, yellowish glaze. It is often decorated with an impressed or moulded design or with lattice work.
- Early Mason's Ironstone can be identified by its mark. Between 1813 and 1815 it had 'Patent Ironstone China' impressed in a circle. The circle was dropped and 'Mason's' added until 1825. From about 1820 printed marks were used.
- Minton majolica has the year it was made marked in symbol form. Majolica wares can be recognized by their rich colours, thick glazes and relief moulding.
- Stoneware is noticeably heavier than earthenware. Broken or chipped pieces have a glassy look.

IDENTIFYING PORCELAIN

HOW TO TELL THE DIFFERENCE BETWEEN SOFT PASTE, HARD PASTE, AND BONE CHINA

There are three types of porcelain – soft paste, hard paste, and bone china. Although they look similar, by spotting small differences in their appearance you will be able to identify which is which.

▼ *Soft-paste wares, like this Worcester creamer, are earlier and often more prized by collectors than hard-paste.* ❹

Soft-paste wares have a warm grainy feel. Often there are scratches on the glaze, and any damaged edges are granular, like a sugar cube. Soft-paste porcelain was first used by European potters in 1738. It was made by mixing white clay with 'frit', a mixture of sand, gypsum, soda, salt, alum, and nitre. Everything was fused together with lime and chalk, and the mixture was fired at a low temperature.

Years of trial and error produced a true European hard-paste porcelain. China clay (kaolin) was mixed with china stone, a stony oxide of aluminium, and the paste stored for seven to eight months to improve the strength and whiteness of the finished porcelain. Because it was fired at very high temperatures, hard-paste porcelain is

◀ *This cup and saucer, typical of soft-paste pieces, has been decorated with rich enamels before being fired.* ❺

hard, glassy and cold to the touch. The glaze will not flake off, and on a broken piece it is hard to tell where the glaze ends and the paste begins.

Bone china combines some of the qualities of hard and soft paste ware: like hard paste porcelain, the glaze is fast, but it has the warm feel of soft paste porcelain. Its paste is a strong mixture of china clay, china stone and calcined animal bone. Because this paste can withstand great heat in the kiln it produces a very translucent and very white type of porcelain.

▲ *Check the translucency of fine bone china by holding it to the light with a finger behind. The finger should be clearly visible.*

◀ *Bone china ware, such as this late Victorian cup and saucer, was first put on the market in the late 18th century.* ❺

CHINESE WARES

Porcelain came originally from China and was first encountered by European traders in the 18th century. Potters in England and France worked hard at reproducing its wonderful, white translucence, so very different from the native, dark earthenware. White or blue and white Chinese wares, like this vase, inspired British potters to create imitation soft-paste porcelain. Although far from a perfect copy of Chinese wares, it did have the same prized translucent apearance.

MAKERS' MARKS

*COLLECTING CHINA IS A REWARDING PASTIME AND, WITH A LITTLE
KNOWLEDGE OF MAKERS' MARKS, YOU CAN MORE ACCURATELY DATE
AND VALUE YOUR CERAMICS*

M ost of us will look at the bottom of a
piece of china when we are browsing
at antique fairs or markets, but few of
us really understand what we see. Marks
on china can be very useful to
the collector – a genuine
mark can help to identify
and date an object, in-
valuable when you are
considering the worth
of a piece of china.
But beware relying
only on the mark;
there are many forg-
eries of famous marks.
Marks can only be re-
lied upon in conjunc-
tion with other informa-
tion, such as the feel of the
piece and the style and kind of
decoration.

The practice of identifying the maker of a
pot by marking the base dates back at least
to Roman times, but the first modern factory mark appeared in 16th-century Europe.
The crossed swords painted on Meissen
porcelain from 1723 helped to spread the practice. In France from 1766 on, porcelain makers were required by law to register a mark,
but elsewhere marks had no official status.

As a result, while top makers usually identified their pieces, others either left their wares
unmarked or shamelessly put on imitations
of famous marks. The Meissen mark, the interlaced Ls of Sèvres, and the crescent of

▲ *This mark is printed.
The Chamberlains fac-
tory was founded in
Worcester in 1783.*

▲ *The crossed swords
of Meissen is perhaps the
most famous mark of all.*

Worcester were all widely copied in the 18th century.

By the 19th century, most potteries had their own system of marking and marks were increasingly applied to all forms of pottery. There was a practical reason for this. The century saw a shift away from fairs and travelling peddlers towards retail stores as a means of selling; retailers used the information in the mark to re-order popular items. As a result, printed marks of the period often contain the name of the pattern and shape as well as that of the maker.

China marks are generally found on the base of items, or in other unseen places, and can be applied to the china in a variety of ways. Impressed marks are those which are stamped into the body of the soft clay before firing; these are virtually impossible to fake. Incised marks are similar to impressed ones except that they are scratched into the clay rather than stamped. Underglaze marks are printed or painted by hand onto the surface of the china before the glaze is applied,and are usually in blue. Overglaze marks are in any colour and are printed , stencilled or painted on after the glaze has been fired.

Makers' marks can help you date china. For instance, some companies changed their names or used different symbols on their ware over the years. If you know at what date these changes occurred, it can help you place a piece of china at a certain period in time.

▲ *The bottom of this jug is well marked. The lion and crown identifies it as Royal Doulton. There is a design number with a D prefix, a 'Dickens' series stamp, while 'Mark Tapley' refers to the Dickens character depicted on the jug.*

◀ *The three wavy blue lines appear on all Royal Copenhagen pieces, while the printed mark was added to pieces made between 1894 and 1922.*

IDENTIFYING CHINA BY SHAPE

SOMETIMES THE SHAPE OF A PIECE OF POTTERY CAN GIVE VALUABLE CLUES TO ITS AGE AND ITS PURPOSE

S hape is one among many factors which can help you to date a piece of pottery. In some pieces it tells very little. Plates for example, have their shape dictated by their function, and have changed little over the centuries. The same is not so true of hollow ware – cups, jugs, teapots and so on – which offers far more scope for variation.

The problem with dating pottery by its shape is that although new types and forms of pottery are continually being introduced, very few of them are completely discontinued. As a result, all that you can say about a teapot with a 'Regency' shape is that it could not have been made much before 1800, though it may well have been created at more or less any time since.

When hot beverages such as tea, coffee and hot chocolate first became popular in the 17th century, they were usually drunk from silver

UP SHAPES

A Regency coffee cup and six tea cups illustrate the extraordinary range of types and sizes possible and the difficulty of putting a date on any of them based only on their shape.

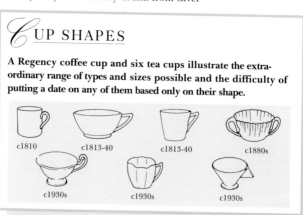

c1810   c1813-40   c1813-40   c1880s

c1930s   c1930s   c1930s

cups. Only in the 18th century did genteel society gradually discover the particular affinity between tea and porcelain.

Early cups either had no handles, in the Chinese style, or they had two. The single handle came into fashion only in the middle of the 18th century.

Cups were usually sold as part of a 'trio', consisting of a coffee cup, a tea cup and a saucer for use with both. Coffee cups were generally taller and narrower than tea cups. Straight-

TEAPOT SHAPES

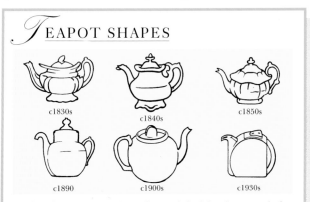

c1830s

c1840s

c1850s

c1890

c1900s

c1930s

Fashions in teapots overlapped a good deal, but in general, they were melon-shaped in the first half of the 19th century, roughly oval in the second half, and more rounded in the 20th century.

sided coffee cups, or cans, were particularly popular from 1800 to 1820.

Pottery teapots were first made in Britain in the early 18th century. The first teapots tended to be globular, with short, straight spouts, and came complete with a stand. They were small because tea was a luxury drink. The majority of tea and coffee was still brewed in silver pots, though, and silver designs were used for china and earthenware pots. Later on in the century, influenced by silver designs, melon-shaped and octagonal pots came into vogue. In the 19th century, standard pots were round or oval with a raised base or feet.

CHINESE PORCELAIN

FOR TWO CENTURIES, CHINA WAS THE WEST'S ONLY SOURCE OF PORCELAIN. EVEN AFTER EUROPEAN FACTORIES DISCOVERED THE SECRET, MOST PORCELAIN SOLD IN EUROPE WAS CHINESE

P ortuguese ships first brought Chinese porcelain to Europe in the 16th century. Its whiteness, translucency and delicacy enchanted westerners. Although a few European factories discovered how to make porcelain of their own in the 18th century, trade in Chinese pieces continued to grow, reaching a peak between 1760 and 1780. By this time the English had taken over from the Portuguese as China's main trading partners.

The underglaze blue of the Kangxi period in the late 17th century was rich and vibrant, and the glaze very smooth and clear, but the

CHINESE STYLE

This covered jar is typical of authentic Chinese ware, rather than that made for export. Made around 1800, it is decorated with green dragons chasing through stylized clouds. Although reign marks on Chinese pieces can be misleading, this one, for Jiaqing (1796-1820), is right for the piece.

▲ *Exotic birds decorate this octagonal* famille verte *dish of c.1700. The small vase is* famille rose, *and was made in 1750 as a spitoon. Both pieces fall within the same price guide.* **9**

Europeans wanted more. Chinese decorators began making polychrome, or multi-coloured, porcelain and by 1720, the demand for it had outstripped that for blue and white.

The earliest polychrome wares used enamel colours, especially green; they're known as *famille verte* (green family). *Famille verte* ware is usually highly coloured and ornate, and decorated with stylized patterns, flowers, birds, fish or scenes from Chinese legend or history. *Famille rose* (pink family), a much softer palette of colours, became popular in the 1730s. As well as traditional designs, many were created specifically for the western market. It was commonplace for aristocrats to order services decorated with their family coat of arms.

Dating pieces of Chinese porcelain can be a problem. Some pieces can be roughly dated by their marks, which usually give the current Emperor's name. However, in 1677 the Emperor decreed his name must not appear on pottery, as to break it would desecrate him. The names of earlier emperors were used instead, mainly for decoration, with no intent to deceive. Some Chinese wares from the 19th century bear reign marks as early as the 1400s.

SEVRES PORCELAIN

THE FORTUNES OF THE FRENCH PORCELAIN FACTORY, SEVRES, IN THE 18TH AND 19TH CENTURY FOLLOWED THOSE OF THE NATION AND PRODUCED TWO PERIODS OF GREAT INFLUENCE

I n 1738, a factory was founded at the Château de Vincennes to manufacture fine soft-paste porcelain for the nobility. It thrived, attracting royal patronage, and was awarded a state monopoly of the manufacture of painted and gilded porcelain wares.

In 1752, Louis XV, influenced by his mistress, Madame de Pompadour, became the major shareholder. Four years later, the factory moved to the town of Sèvres, and in 1759 Louis took over completely.

▼ *This jug, covered with gilt, has a panel depicting the Château de Vincennes, where the Sèvres factory was set up in 1738.* ❿

Sèvres led France, and indeed Europe, in producing luxury ornamental table wares. The light, delicate, creamy porcelain featured rich, enamelled ground colours enclosing white panels painted with delicate bird and flower studies or landscapes. The panel borders were often elaborate and liberal use was made of gilding.

The French Revolution (1789) swept away much of Sèvres' aristocratic clientele. After the factory was nationalized in 1793, its stock was sold off to be decorated elsewhere. A new director took over the moribund works in 1800. He abandoned the making of soft-paste porcelain for hard-paste, introduced there in the 1760s. Sèvres won huge orders from the Napoleonic government in the new Empire style. Further reorganization in 1848 led to a switch in emphasis from decoration to the quality of the porcelain itself. Much

COMPARE & CONTRAST

Earlier Sèvres work, represented here by one of the factory's reproduction plates (*bottom*), was paler in colour, with finer gilding and naturalistic decoration. The neoclassical style of the Empire period was characterized by heavy gilding on a dark ground. The cameo figure in classical dress in the centre of the plate (*top*) is a typical decorative motif of the time.

paler colours were used. The factory moved to St-Cloud in 1876, and continues there today. Apart from some fine work in the Art Nouveau and Art Deco styles, much of the production in the last 100 years has been copies or smaller versions of wares from the 18th century.

The Sèvres style inspired other porcelain makers from the beginning. Some made honest reproductions, others downright forgeries. All Sèvres marks should be treated with a large pinch of salt. Experts estimate that as many as 95 per cent of marked 'Sèvres' pieces did not originate in the factory. Style and quality of decoration are a better guide, but it often takes an expert to tell the difference. In the 19th century, Minton of England produced classic Sèvres reproductions to a very high standard. Today, they are valued almost as much as the originals.

▲ *The famous Sèvres mark of the 18th century had a date code between two interlaced Ls.*

EARLY FRENCH PORCELAIN

THOUGH THE SEVRES FACTORY DOMINATED PORCELAIN PRODUCTION IN FRANCE IN THE 18TH AND 19TH CENTURIES, OTHER FACTORIES TRIED HARD TO EMULATE ITS SUCCESS

I n the 1770s, following the relaxation of laws giving Sèvres a monopoly on porcelain manufacture, several factories opened in Paris. The biggest name among them was that of La Courtille, which was in production from 1771 to around 1840. All the factories used hard-paste porcelain and the majority made only tableware, leaving elaborate neo-classical vases, urns and other ornamental china to Sèvres. None of them developed their own style however but were content to imitate Sèvres.

The main porcelain centre outside Paris was at Limoges, close to the main sources of kaolin and other minerals used in the making of

◀ *These teaset pieces were made by the Limoges factory around 1820. The price guide applies to the full set.* 🎱

porcelain. Other factories moved or were established there in the 19th century and today it is the chief centre of porcelain production in France.

Those who enjoy the decorative porcelain produced by Sèvres in the 18th and early 19th century, but find it too expensive, could do worse than pick up the similar, much cheaper pieces produced in Paris and Limoges. Single items from tea and dinner services can be found at quite reasonable prices.

Many factories did not mark their wares, however, and the crossed Ls of Sèvres were often added later. The La Courtille factory is an exception: its products, many of which were pirated from figures modelled at Sèvres, carried their own mark of crossed torches or arrows painted in underglaze blue. Another important factory, set up in 1795 by the Darte brothers in the Rue de Charonne, made fine Sèvres copies with the painted signature Darte Frères.

▲ *This sauce tureen was made in Paris in about 1815. It is one of a pair and the price guide is for both.* **9**

▼ *A simple pattern in rust and gilt decorates this cup and saucer of around 1820.* **4**

21

EARLY BRITISH PORCELAIN

BETWEEN THE MID-18TH AND THE MID-19TH CENTURIES, THE BRITISH PORCELAIN AND BONE CHINA INDUSTRY PRODUCED A HUGE RANGE OF EXTREMELY COLLECTABLE WARES

The whiteness, translucence and 'ring' of Chinese porcelain was so obviously superior to the other forms of pottery that were available in 17th and 18th century Europe that hundreds of potters devoted their lives to discovering its secret.

The first breakthrough came in the London area in the 1740s, when factories at Bow and Chelsea produced soft-paste porcelain wares. The first hard-paste factory was established at Plymouth in 1768 to take advantage of the china clay deposits that had recently been discovered not far away in Cornwall. The other main category of porcelain, bone china (hard paste plus bone ash), was patented by Josiah Spode in

▲ *This Coalport side plate has a combination of colours that is typical of the first half of the 19th century.* ❹

DEALERS' TIPS

• **Cobalt blue was not widely available in Britain until the end of the Napoleonic wars in 1815, when it could be imported from Saxony.**
• **Look on makers' marks as guides rather than guarantees. The thickness and colour of the glaze is often a better guide.**
• **In soft-paste porcelain, colours tend to fuse with the glaze; the decoration on hard-paste is generally crisper.**

*D*ECORATION

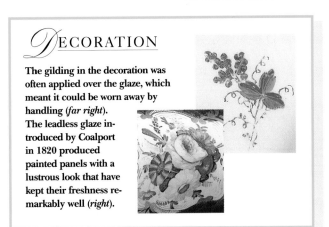

The gilding in the decoration was often applied over the glaze, which meant it could be worn away by handling (*far right*). The leadless glaze introduced by Coalport in 1820 produced painted panels with a lustrous look that have kept their freshness remarkably well (*right*).

1794. Bone china remains a British speciality. Whatever the type, 18th-century British porcelain, which included both useful and decorative wares, was greatly influenced by the top European factories – particularly Meissen in Germany and Sèvres in France – and by Chinese decorative styles.

In the first decades of the 19th century, the manufacture of porcelain, and particularly of bone china, was a thriving industry in England. The factory at Worcester was pre-eminent, but fine wares were also being produced by Coalport, Derby, Minton, Rockingham, Spode and Wedgwood. Of these, only Rockingham, which closed in 1842, is no longer in business.

The Worcester factory was probably the best, and certainly the most long-lived of the 18th-century porcelain makers. In the 1790s a rival factory in Worcester started making hard-paste porcelain of its own; the two companies were merged in 1840 under the name Chamberlain & Co. These Worcester factories excelled at tableware with fine, hand-painted decoration.

▲ *This Coalport breakfast cup of the 1820s has its price reduced by a crack near the handle.* **5**

23

WEDGWOOD BLACK BASALTE

*THE RICH BLACK STONEWARES PERFECTED BY JOSIAH WEDGWOOD
IN THE 1770S CAUGHT THE POPULAR IMAGINATION AND WERE
WIDELY COPIED BY OTHER STAFFORDSHIRE FACTORIES*

J osiah Wedgwood was the premier figure in 18th-century pottery making.
In 1769 he opened a new factory in
partnership with Thomas Bentley. The Etruria
works was the largest pottery in the world at
the time, and was dedicated to producing ornamental wares in a fine, unglazed black
stoneware that Wedgwood called Black Basalte.
Black Basalte wares were based on Roman,
Greek and Etruscan originals, and fitted in
perfectly with the neo-classical style that was
the dominant fashion for interior design in
the 1770s.

*▼Ancient Egypt was
an important influence
in the 1800s, when this
sphinx candleholder
was made.* **7**

Vases and ewers were the mainstay
of production at Wedgwood's Etruria
factory, but the range also included many useful wares, such
as candleholders, lamps, baskets,
flowerpots, ink stands, mugs and
teapots. Busts were also produced,
some of them copied from classsical
examples and others modelled
from life or from painted
portraits. The instant
success of the new
Wedgwood range
prompted other
Staffordshire pot-
ters to produce
black basalt wares –
among the better of these
factories were Spode and Neale.

Early Wedgwood pieces were ornamented
with encaustic decoration, where the painted
colours were literally burned on during fir-

ing. Red was the favourite colour, though white was also used. The decoration features thin lines and lies flush with the surface of the piece. Later, Wedgwood and its competitors alike achieved similar effects with the technique of moulding low relief decoration in coloured clays and applying it to the pots with a solution of slip. Although most unglazed stonewares have a matt finish, basalt ware was capable of developing a high polish as it was dusted and handled over the years, and could somtimes resemble bronze.

Wedgwood Black Basalte ware made after 1780 carries the familiar WEDGWOOD mark (*see page 27*). Do not confuse this with marks such as Wedgewood and J. Wedgwood, made by John Wedge Wood, WEDGEWOOD & CO., and other fakes used to mislead buyers.

Basalt wares had their greatest popularity in the first half of the 19th century, but the appeal of this stoneware has proved as durable as its body, and the Wedgwood company still makes it today. Because black basalt wares last so well, pieces from the late 18th and early 19th centuries have survived in some numbers. As Josiah Wedgwood himself claimed 'The black is sterling and will last forever'.

▲ *Early Wedgwood pieces are decorated with encaustic decoration (top), as opposed to the later technique of relief moulding (bottom).*

▼ *Made around 1800, this Wedgwood butter dish has its decoration applied in terracotta moulding.* ❼

WEDGWOOD JASPER WARE

JASPER WARE, MADE ALMOST CONTINUOUSLY FOR THE LAST 200 YEARS, IS SO CHARACTERISTIC THAT IT IS OFTEN KNOWN SIMPLY AS WEDGWOOD

J osiah Wedgwood founded his pottery in 1759 but it was not until 1774, after several years of disappointment and about 3,000 recorded experiments, that he felt he had produced his decorative masterpiece, and Jasper ware first appeared on the market.

This dense, white, unglazed stoneware was fired at a higher than usual temperature so that it resembled porcelain. It was made in various colours – light and dark blue, lilac, green, yellow and black – obtained either by adding a ground colour to the solid body, or by staining. Various shades of blue were the most popular colours, including the sky blue now known as Wedgwood blue.

Jasper ware was an immediate, resounding success. The pale colours, in particular, suited the light, airy, neo-classical style that

▲ *A design known as 'the dancing hours' decorates this urn, which has been dipped in lilac stain.* ❼

◀ *Slight discolouration reduces the price of this blue Jasper plate.* ❼

was popular at the time. The majority of pieces were decorated with low reliefs based on Greek and Roman decorative styles. The reliefs were often designed by famous artists of the day. They were separately moulded in white Jasper then applied to the piece.

Many fine copies of Jasper ware were made by other Staffordshire potters from very soon after Josiah Wedgwood introduced it. Some of the best were made by William Adams of Tunstall. Much early imitation Jasper was well-produced and the relief work finely executed. Slight variations of the impressed Wedgwood mark were rife.

▼ *The impressed mark in capital letters has been used by the factory since 1759.*

Although the fashion for the classical has waxed and waned over the last two centuries, Jasper ware has gone from strength to strength, and is still being made at the Wedgwood factory.

$\mathcal{C}$OMPARE & CONTRAST

The sugar box on the left is a fine copy of Wedgwood's Jasper ware. Produced by William Adams around 1800, it is betrayed by the vividness of the blue, as compared with the modern Wedgwood bowl on the right.

EARLY CREAMWARE

FIRST DEVELOPED AS A CHEAP BUT USEFUL ALTERNATIVE TO PORCELAIN, CREAMWARE SOON BECAME POPULAR IN ITS OWN RIGHT

While many 18th century potters devoted their lives to recreating the glories of Chinese porcelain, others attempted to provide a more affordable ware as a substitute. The aim among Staffordshire potters was to make earthenware that was cheap, robust and had the look of porcelain. The results would fall short of one of these three aims until 1761, when Josiah Wedgwood perfected creamware, a type of earthenware with a strong, near-white body and a thick, yellowish glaze.

In 1765 Wedgwood was commissioned to supply Queen Charlotte with a 60-piece creamware tea set. The result was so admired that Wedgwood was appointed 'Potter to Her Majesty' and Wedgwood creamware was known from then on as Queen's Ware.

The enormous success of creamware led Wedgwood to experiment with vases and other purely decorative articles, while other potteries – particularly those at Leeds, Liverpool and Swansea – produced creamware services and decorative items of their own.

A great deal of cream-coloured tableware was sold without applied decoration of any kind. In many other instances, ornament was restricted to pierced borders, fretwork and

▲ *A transfer print of a ship decorates the centre of this dinner plate from a service made around 1790.* ❺

28

lattice decoration or to simple floral or geometric borders. However, some articles, especially teapots, jugs and punch bowls, may have quite elaborate transfer-printed or enamel-painted decoration. It is the quality of the decoration that largely sets creamware prices.

Creamware has been made continuously, by Wedgwood and others, for more than 200 years and is still being made today. Dating it can only be done by experience – develop a feel by seeing and handling as many pieces as possible.

Although the rich, buttery finish of early creamware had its admirers in the 18th century, the majority of customers seem to have regarded paleness as a sign of quality. Something of this remains today, making early creamware surprisingly available and affordable.

▲ *This creamware urn, decorated with a fret pattern, was probably intended for serving fruit or nuts.* **5**

CREAMWARE DECORATION

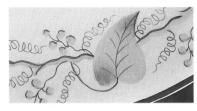

The border of the early Queen's Ware plate (*above*) has been painted entirely by hand, whereas the jug decoration (*above right*) has a black transfer print which has been overpainted by hand. Decorative moulding (*right*) was common on early creamware.

BLUE-WHITE PEARLWARE

PLAIN WHITE WITH JUST A HINT OF BLUE, PEARLWARE WAS, AFTER CREAMWARE, BLACK BASALTE AND JASPER WARE, THE FOURTH TYPE OF EARTHENWARE TO BE DEVELOPED BY JOSIAH WEDGWOOD

A lthough Wedgwood had perfected creamware in 1761, he still sought to re-create the blue-white moonlit look of the best Chinese porcelain in earthenware. In 1779, Wedgwood marketed the results of his experiments as Pearl White ware, later known more simply as pearlware. The new ware was a first cousin to creamware; the only differences were that the body contained more white clay and flint, and was fired at a higher temperature, while a small amount of cobalt was added to give a hint of blue to the glaze.

Wedgwood himself was not as committed to the new style as he was to his other innovations – he made it clear that he was simply responding to fashionable taste, declaring that 'the pearl white ware must be considered a change rather than an improvement'.

The white body with a faint blue tinge made pearlware ideal for blue and white designs in the Chinese style, and from 1790 until about 1820, pearlware was the base for

▲ *This 1780 pearlware coffee pot shows the uneven glaze sometimes seen on early pieces.* ❺

◀ *The decoration of this pearlware goblet shows a Japanese influence.* ❺

30

most Staffordshire blue and white earthenware, usually transfer-printed under the glaze. It was rarely left undecorated, as creamware often was.

After about 1820, pearlware gradually drifted out of fashion, and Wedgwood ceased production in 1846. Other factories, though, continued to make pearlware.

▲ *The quintal vase is an unusual shape for any ware, and this, along with the charming hand-painted design, makes up for the obvious damage.* ❻

𝒟EALERS' TIPS

• **Painted pieces generally cost more than those that have been transfer-printed or left with only minimal decoration.**
• **Small useful wares tend to cost the least, while decorative wares such as figures, pots pourris and large vases tend to be more pricey.**
• **Well-marked Wedgwood pieces, particularly ones from the late 18th century, attract the most money.**

BIEDERMEIER PORCELAIN

WITH ITS SIMPLE, CLEAN OUTLINES AND ELEGANT NEO-CLASSICAL DECORATION, BIEDERMEIER PORCELAIN GRACED THE HOMES OF THE PROSPEROUS MIDDLE CLASSES

From the early 19th century, porcelain factories in Germany and Austria began producing a range of wares that were considerably plainer than the grand services ordered by royalty but more sumptuous than the everyday tableware used in the ordinary home.

◀ *A cup and saucer from the Vienna factory gives the illusion of having precious stones embedded in its body.* **8**

This was Biedermeier porcelain, and, as the century progressed, it was to be seen increasingly frequently in the homes of the comfortable middle classes. Indeed the term Biedermeier comes from a fictional character called Gottlieb Biedermeier, who personified the solid, unpretentious tastes of the middle classes in the early 19th century.

Porcelain of this period represents a simplified version of the neo-classical style which

▼ *Decoration included classical motifs, as well as subjects from the natural world.*

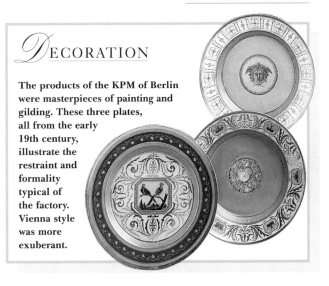

DECORATION

The products of the KPM of Berlin were masterpieces of painting and gilding. These three plates, all from the early 19th century, illustrate the restraint and formality typical of the factory. Vienna style was more exuberant.

had dominated European art for half a century. The finest Biedermeier porcelain was made in Vienna by the Royal Imperial Porcelain Factory and in Berlin by the Königliche Porzellan Manufaktur (Royal Porcelain Factory) or KPM.

Most pieces bear a factory mark, the only sure means of identification. The Berlin mark is simply the initials KPM, occasionally accompanied by an orb, a sceptre or an eagle. The Vienna factory's mark is a shield with two horizontal bars drawn across it.

The fine decoration on Biedermeier meant that the porcelain was increasingly likely to be made for display rather than use. A wide range of colours was used for naturalistic animal and flower paintings, portraits and scenic views. Landscapes and townscapes are particularly associated with Biedermeier porcelain; vistas, squares, opera houses, cathedrals and gardens in Vienna, Berlin and other cities were exactingly reproduced. Whereas painters on porcelain had once remained anonymous, artists of the Biedermeier period enjoyed rising status.

STAFFORDSHIRE FIGURES

IN THE 19TH CENTURY, SMALL, HOLLOW EARTHENWARE FIGURES WERE MADE IN HUGE QUANTITIES BY STAFFORDSHIRE POTTERIES

S taffordshire potteries produced enormous numbers of full-length, portrait figures in Victorian times. They were responding to an upsurge in public demand for cheap but colourful ornaments that reflected the general increase in prosperity in Britain throughout the century.

While pre-Victorian Staffordshire figures had been well crafted and highly coloured in an attempt to imitate porcelain, Victorian potters had no such lofty ambitions. They simply set out to give the public what it wanted as cheaply as possible. They took their inspiration wherever they could find it, copying illustrations from coloured prints, broadsheets, newspapers and magazines of the day. The figures rarely cost more than a few pence when new, but have appreciated enormously in value in the last few decades as they are more and more recognized as pieces of charming and decorative folk art.

The manufacturing process began with a modeller who made an original figure out of clay. A master mould was taken from this clay model and further moulds were

▲ *Napoleon Bonaparte was the subject of more figures than any other person.* ❼

◀ *The bridle and mane of this 1850 zebra show that it was made from a horse mould.* ❼

◀ *This musical couple, made about 1860, are shown wearing historical costume as they duet on pipes and lute. The price is for the pair.* **6**

then taken from the master mould. They were made in two halves, front and back.

The clay was pressed into the moulds quite thinly with a sponge; the edges were coated with slip and the two halves were bound tightly together. The plaster absorbed the moisture from the clay, which was removed from the mould, hand-finished and put in the kiln. It was then painted and glazed. One of the most popular colours was a rich cobalt blue. For technical reasons, this was rarely used after 1863.

Staffordshire figures were often made and sold in pairs and this is particularly true of the animals. Made as right-hand and left-hand examples, they were intended to be displayed on either side of the hearth.

▼ *Usually sold in pairs, comforter dogs were among the most popular Staffordshire animals.* **6**

CROWN DERBY FIGURES

THE FIGURES PRODUCED BY THE CROWN DERBY FACTORY ARE AMONG THE MOST COLLECTABLE PIECES OF BRITISH PORCELAIN

P orcelain has been made in Derby for around 250 years, since the first factory was opened in the middle of the 18th century. The factory received the Royal Warrant in 1775, which gave it the right to use the crown mark on its wares. After a decline in its fortunes in the first half of the 19th century, a new, much bigger factory was opened in 1875. The traditions of early Derby porcelain were revived, and the company was again granted the Royal Warrant by Queen Victoria in 1890, after which it was known as Royal Crown Derby.

The high quality of potting and decoration has made Derby porcelain collectable from the very beginning. This is particularly true of the figures and figure groups. Those made at the original factory were inspired by the

◀ *This unknown singer with an outflung arm imitates the style of Meissen figures. Delicate decorative figures in pale pastel colours were often made by the Derby factories.* ❾

products of the Meissen factory in Germany – the factory advertised itself as 'the second Dresden'. The figures were decorated in pale pastel colours.

Figures are still made by Royal Crown Derby today, and new ones have been continually added to the range, in both traditional and contemporary styles. This was particularly true between the wars, when figures modelled in a loose Art Deco style were very popular. The most collectable of these are the ones designed by accomplished modellers such as Tom Wilkinson, Arnold Mikelson or Edward Drew.

▲ *These two 18th-century pieces show elaborate detail in modelling and decoration. The price guide is the same for both.* **9**

◄ *This 1940s' study was modelled by Arnold Mikelson.* **6**

DANISH TABLE CHINA

THE ROYAL COPENHAGEN FACTORY, FAMED WORLDWIDE FOR ITS FINE ORNAMENTAL WARES, HAS ALSO PRODUCED A GREAT DEAL OF TABLEWARE IN ITS LONG HISTORY

Denmark is the home of the Royal Copenhagen factory, which has been producing very fine ceramics for over 200 years. The first factory in the city was founded in 1722 to make blue and white pottery. It closed in 1770, but another pottery had been set up in 1755, producing soft-paste porcelain. A new factory was founded in 1775 to make hard-paste porcelain. Three wavy blue lines, representing the three water-ways which surround and divide the country, were adopted as the factory mark (*see page 13*). In 1779 the factory was bought by the King and was known from then on as the Royal Danish Porcelain Factory.

▲ *This selection is taken from a 'full-lace' Blue-Fluted service introduced in the 1880s. The price guide is for all six items.* **9**

COMPARE & CONTRAST

The Blue-Fluted pattern is one of the most imitated in the history of ceramics. In the genuine Royal Danish piece (*above left*), the colour tends to sink into the body. When the pattern is copied (*above right*), it tends to be done over the glaze, giving more contrast in the colours.

The factory's reputation largely rests on two smoky underglaze blue patterns, introduced in the 1770s. One of them, known as the Blue-Fluted pattern, was inspired by an ancient Chinese motif, and was very labour-intensive. Over 1,000 brush-strokes were needed to decorate each plate. Between them, these two patterns have been responsible for more than 90 per cent of the factory's total output. The lacework patterns on the edges, sometimes pierced through, sometimes closed, are a speciality of the factory.

Another famous pattern, the Flora Danica, was introduced in the 1880s. It was first used on an 1,800-piece service commissioned by Danish royalty for Catherine II of Russia, and featured drawings of native Danish plants on a white or cream porcelain ground. Each and every part of the service had its own plant, copied from colour plates with a then unprecedented degree of botanical accuracy.

▼ *This tureen is made in the Flora Danica pattern, with moulded details and gilt rims.* **9**

MASON'S IRONSTONE

FIRST SOLD IN THE EARLY 19TH CENTURY AS AN ALTERNATIVE TO PORCELAIN, MASON'S IRONSTONE CHINA SOON WON CUSTOMERS WITH ITS ATTRACTIVE ENAMELLED DECORATION

Mason's Ironstone, a strong, hard-wearing stoneware that imitated the shapes and decoration of 18th-century porcelain, was developed in the early 19th century by Miles Mason, a Staffordshire porcelain manufacturer. Although it was a stoneware, it became the 'household china' of the aspiring middle classes who could not afford porcelain for everyday use.

The name 'Mason's Patent Ironstone China' proved to be a masterstroke, conjuring up both the strength of stoneware and the refinement of porcelain.

The ware amply fulfilled its name. Made from a whitish clay mixed with a powdered glassy slag, it was smooth, slightly translucent, but robust. When tapped with a fingernail, it gave off a satisfying metallic ring. It was also richly colourful and sold for an affordable retail price. These features made it an instant success.

The basic decoration was transfer-printed onto the body of the ware and then given a protective glaze. Pieces were hand-coloured

▲ *Octagonal jugs were a speciality of the factory, often sold in sets. This jug is in the Fenton shape and was made around 1840.* ❻

DEALERS' TIPS

• From 1813 to 1815 it had 'Patent Ironstone China' impressed within a circle. From 1815 to 1825, 'Mason's Patent Ironstone China' was impressed in one, two or three lines.
• From just before 1820, a printed crown with 'Mason's' above and 'Patent Ironstone China' below was also introduced.

with bright enamels – luminous greens, blues and reds, together with subtler washes – then finished with rich decorative gilding.

The designs were usually all-over patterns, most of them derived from oriental themes, but various European designs, including Italianate landscapes, were also used.

From 1813 to about 1830, the quality of potting and decoration was high. After a period of decline, the factory was sold in 1848. Many of the moulds and printing plates were acquired by members of the Ashworth family who created renewed interest in the ware and ran the business from 1862 until 1968. In 1973 Mason's Patent Ironstone China became part of the Wedgwood group. It is still being made today.

▲ *This elaborate sweetmeat dish is decorated with the Table and Flower Pot pattern.* **7**

▲ *Ashworth & Bros continued to use the Ironstone name when they took over the company in 1862.*

▼ *The iron red and black of this soup tureen made up a popular colour combination.* **6**

41

PARIAN BUSTS & FIGURES

*PARIAN, A FINE SOFT-PASTE PORCELAIN
INTRODUCED IN THE MID-19TH CENTURY, WAS
A POPULAR MEDIUM FOR BUSTS AND STATUES*

W ealthy households could afford genuine marble statuary, but most people made do with imitations. Busts made of plaster of Paris were a popular choice, but a new, fine-grained and unglazed type of porcelain, Parian, which had a slight sheen, was considered much classier.

The new material was introduced in the 1840s by the firm of Copeland & Garrett, closely followed by Minton. Parian had a creamy, off-white surface with a delicacy reminiscent of marble from the Greek island, Paros, hence the name, which was coined by Minton. Many

▲ *This classical nymph
has been clothed in
glazed white Parian.* ❼

other firms made Parian, the most prolific being Robinson & Leadbeater.

Parian was used for vases, flower holders, brooches, inkstands, butter dishes and fruit comports, but was mainly seen in the form of statues, busts, and figure groups, many of them the work of famous sculptors and artists. Parian figures were usually copies.

The fine, crisp detail seen in Parian ware was produced by the enormous shrinkage the material went through when it was fired. The best Parian paste was made of felspar, china clay and a glassy frit. On occasions, the frit was left out of the paste, but this made it unsuitable for statues, although it was fine for tableware. Sometimes the pastes were tinted with blue, green or terracotta slip. The ground of Wedgwood's famous Jasper ware is basically coloured Parian.

▲ *This portrait of Queen Victoria's consort, PrinceAlbert, was made and sold by Copeland in 1862.* **8**

ℐIGNIFICANT DETAILS

Good Parian models are characterized by fine, detailed modelling, which takes on an extra sharpness during firing.

Details of jewellery or clothing are sometimes emphasized with discreet dabs of gilding. Parian pieces usually have marks on the back or the underside of the base: the sculptor's name may appear, as well as the name of the piece and the maker's mark.

43

BELLEEK
PORCELAIN

FOR MORE THAN 100 YEARS, THE BELLEEK PORCELAIN FACTORY IN
IRELAND HAS BEEN FAMOUS FOR ITS DELICATELY MODELLED
PARIAN WARES AND ITS IRIDESCENT GLAZES

I n 1857, a factory was founded in the small town of
Belleek in County
Fermanagh, Ireland.
There were extensive
deposits of china clay
(kaolin) and felspar,
the main ingredi-
ents of fine porce-
lain, in the area. The
factory was soon
making a range of
decorative Parian
wares (*see page 42*)
which gained it a
world-wide reputation.
Unlike other Parian
wares, however, many of the
products of the Belleek factory
had a complete or partial iridescent
glaze, and some were hand-coloured.

Busts and statues were the natural medium for Parian, which looked like marble, but
Belleek made many other wares, including
elaborate table centrepieces and vases, extremely light tea services, brooches, ornaments,
lamps and mirror frames, jugs and jardinières, wall brackets and dessert services.
All display great delicacy of modelling, and
many have a nautical theme, with motifs based
on shells, fish, coral, sea urchins and so on.

Perhaps the most characteristic Belleek
pieces, though, are the baskets. The basic weave
was painstakingly built up in a woven lattice
of two, three, or, from 1921, four thin strands

▲ *This 'Sydenham*
twig' basket has applied
roses round the edge
and dates from 1870. **9**

▶ *This 'Tea for Two' set*
has a pattern based on sea
urchins and coral. **8**

of clay, and was usually finished off with applied, sometimes coloured flowers.

From the beginning, Belleek wares have been marked by the quality of the modelling and by the dramatic use of clear, shining glazes, with perhaps just a hint of colour. Its fortunes have waxed and waned over the years but, under Irish-American ownership, it is still producing Parian wares today. The great majority of Belleek products carry a clear printed mark featuring a seated Irish wolfhound looking back over its left shoulder, a round tower and an Irish harp above the name of the factory.

The mark gives you a broad guide to dating. The words 'Co Fermanagh Ireland' did not appear until 1891, and were replaced by just the name of the country in 1965. In 1926, a circle was added beneath the banner, containing the Gaelic legend, 'Deanta in Eirinn' (Made in Ireland). A capital R in a circle was added to the trade mark in 1955; this was placed to the right of the harp until 1965, and has been above ever since. The mark was printed in black until 1946, in green from 1946 to 1981, and in gold from 1981.

Beacuse of the intricacy of the pieces you should examine them very carefully before buying to make sure that nothing has been broken off. A missing leaf or petal, for instance, is easily overlooked and can affect the price.

▲ *Elaborate flower modelling makes this tall vase a very desirable item.* ❾

BLUE AND WHITE CHINA

WITH ITS AMAZINGLY VARIED AND LAVISHLY PRINTED DESIGNS,
BLUE AND WHITE TRANSFER-PRINTED CHINA IS AS POPULAR
TODAY AS IT WAS IN VICTORIAN TIMES

Blue and white transfer-printed china was first produced at the end of the 18th century and was so popular that, even today, nearly everyone has at least one piece. Previously, most blue and white ceramics were imported at great expense from China. The price of hand-painted pieces put them out of the range of most people's pockets. When British firms found a way to undercut the Chinese wares, the market boomed.

The transfer-printing technique involved making an engraving of the chosen pattern on a copper plate. This was then used to make a print on tissue. The paper was pressed on to the plain white china, before being floated off, leaving the pattern 'transferred'. The piece was then dipped in transparent glaze and fired. Because pottery was easier and less expensive

▲ *This teapot, dating from around 1800, has a pattern inspired by Chinese motifs.* **6**

*M*AKERS' MARKS

These marks all denote wares from the Spode factory, but at different times during its history.

to produce than porcelain, it provided the ideal material for this new decorating technique. The most popular colour was always blue, but transfer-printed wares can also be found in pink, green, red, black and sepia. These colours were over-glaze, however, as blue was the only colour which could withstand the high firing temperature for underglaze decoration.

The most commonly found English blue and white china is dinnerware. The tough glaze protected the pattern from knife-and-fork damage and the flat surfaces of the plates provided an ideal 'canvas' for the scenic views that became so popular. It was produced in vast quantities during the 19th century, when a dinner service was made up of a vast array of different plates.

Names to look for on blue and white china are Josiah Spode, Enoch Wood, James & Ralph Clews, Davenport, John Rogers, Copeland & Garrett, Wedgwood and Minton. The fact that a piece is not marked does not necessarily affect its value; it is common with early pieces.

▲ *Windmills were commonplace in the 1820s, when this plate was made. It has particularly good engraving.* **6**

✳MISMATCHED PATTERNS

Patterns which do not quite match up indicate where one transfer ends and another begins. Even the best makers occasionally made a mistake. This detail is from a fleur-de-lys Copeland plate, dating from 1852 but worth only £18.

WILLOW PATTERN CHINA

OF ALL THE CHINOISERIE DESIGNS THAT WERE PRODUCED IN BRITAIN IN THE 18TH CENTURY, NONE HAS HAD THE SAME SUCCESS AND ENDURING APPEAL AS WILLOW PATTERN

◀ *This late Victorian platter is similar to thousands produced at the end of the last century as attractive and affordable tableware.* ❹

T he most popular design ever used to decorate tableware was first used on blue and white china. It was known as the Willow Pattern, and the story attached to it (*see facing page*) was invented around 1800 by the Regency equivalent of an advertising copywriter to explain the basic elements of an extremely successful design for decorating pottery.

Traditional Willow Pattern has a pagoda or tea house centre right, a bridge with two or three running figures on it on the left, a boat above the bridge, and, beyond that, the youth's island home. Two doves fly above and in the foreground are two trees, one either a cherry, apple or orange, and the other a willow. A densely patterned blue border surrounds the scene.

Though many of the decorative motifs were copied from Chinese painted porcelain, the Willow Pattern itself was

▲ *The bowl of this sauce ladle from the 1830s shows part of the Willow Pattern.* ❺

48

THE WILLOW PATTERN STORY

Once upon a time, a young Chinese girl was betrothed to a rich but elderly merchant. The girl, though, had lost her heart to a young man and so the young lovers eloped. They fled across a bridge, pursued by the girl's father, and escaped in a boat. They were soon caught, and threatened with death for their crimes, but the gods took pity on them; they were transformed into turtle-doves and flew away together.

essentially an English creation. The definitive version of it was produced by the Spode factory around 1810.

At first, Willow Pattern was almost always seen on useful wares such as tea and dinner services, but later was applied to just about everything, from candleholders to cutlery handles and cow creamers. Potters elsewhere in Europe produced their own version of Willow Pattern, and in the 20th century, factories in the USA and Japan also copied it.

The great majority of wares were transfer-printed in blue, though prints in other colours, a few pieces painted in underglaze blue and polychrome versions of the pattern were also produced. None had the same commercial appeal as the basic blue and white. The pattern is widely collected, particularly in the United States, where there are several flourishing collectors' clubs.

▼ *The early date, around 1815, of this dessert dish, as well as its unusual shape, add to its value.* ❺

49

GLITTERING LUSTREWARE

PROVING THAT ALL THAT GLITTERS IS NOT GOLD, THE METALLIC GLEAM OF LUSTREWARE POTTERY HAS DELIGHTED CHINA COLLECTORS SINCE EARLY IN THE 19TH CENTURY

L ustre is a finish applied to pottery that gives it a metallic sheen. Ranging in use from all-over application to fine details, lustreware has been popular for almost 200 years. Although metallic lustres were used in medieval Europe, by the 1800s lustreware was an exclusively English ceramic.

During the 19th century, many potteries produced all-over lustreware, sometimes gold, but more commonly silver. Many silver pieces were direct copies of traditional silver designs, such as tea sets and candlesticks, and were sold as cheaper alternatives. But by the 1840s and the invention of electroplating, cheap silver plate became available and the manufacture of silver lustreware declined. Throughout the Victorian era, however, gold and silver lustre

▲ *This Staffordshire jug from c.1850 is decorated mainly with copper lustre; the orange bands have a resist pattern on them.* ❻

◀ *This silver lustre teapot is decorated in a delicate resist pattern that was used from 1810 onwards.* ❻

continued to be used for decorative detail, particularly on jugs and mugs.

The technique known as resist lustreware was most commonly used on a cream or white glazed earthenware but sometimes blue, canary yellow or rose backgrounds can be found, though examples of these are rare and more valuable. Copper lustre, which is found on a hard red-brown clay body, was scarce until 1823, but from then on it was often used as broad, banded patterns on both mugs and jugs.

▲ *The borders of this Staffordshire milk jug are in pink lustre, as is the wavy line that winds through the finely painted pattern.* ❺

The quality and quantity of gold used in a lustre finish affected the final colour, as did the colour of the pottery to which it was applied. A convincing gold effect was achieved with two or more coats of lustre over a reddish-brown glazed body. Pink tones were created by adding a small amount of tin to the mixture, painted over a white ground. Silver lustre was made by using platinum, though it is always called 'silver' because of the final effect. Because of platinum's higher value, silver lustreware is rarer and more sought after than gold.

$\mathcal{D}$ECORATION

In resist ware (*top*), a pattern was covered with glycerine that would 'resist' the lustre coating. The glycerine evaporated during firing, leaving the pattern free of lustre. The splashed, or mottled, lustre effect (*bottom*) was achieved by making bubbles of oil in the lustre which exploded during firing to leave a mottled appearance.

FRENCH FAIENCE

*AN ENORMOUS AMOUNT OF COLOURFUL FAIENCE HAS BEEN
PRODUCED BY FRENCH POTTERIES IN THE LAST 400 YEARS,
MAKING IT A VERY VARIED FIELD FOR TODAY'S COLLECTORS*

Tin-glazed earthenware is known in
France as faïence. The name derives
from the Italian town of Faenza, which
was famous for its potteries. Migrant Italian
potters made their way to France, bringing
with them the techniques of making
maiolica (the Italian name for the same
product). The bright and colourful
wares were very popular. The most important early French faïence factories,
or *faïenceries*, which flourished from the
beginning of the 17th century, were
based in the towns of Nevers,
Moustiers and Rouen.

At the end of the 18th century,
Nevers produced a series of
plates giving a potted history of
the French revolution. Such
wares, known as *faïence patrio-
tique*, showed Frenchmen wearing Phrygian caps, the soft conical hats that were a symbol of
liberty. These were painted in yellow, as the shade of red they were
in reality was impossible to repro-
duce on pottery. The plates were copied by
other *faïenceries* in the 19th century.

The Moustiers factory was renowned for
its grotesque decoration depicting half-human,
half-animal figures, while at Marseilles, faïence
produced under Veuve Perrin (Widow Perrin)
was famous for its delicate painting.

The faïence industry went into a decline in
the early 19th century. However, later the same
century, there was a great revival. This was

▲ *This grotesque fig-
ure, one of a pair of
candlesticks, is marked
'Rouen'; this denotes the
pattern rather than the
factory. They were actu-
ally made at Desvres.* ❼

largely the result of the increased spending power of the growing middle classes.

Established factories were given a new lease of life and new ones, using mass-production techniques, opened all over France, including ones at Angoulême, Blois, Boulogne, Desvres, Malicorne and Quimper. There is a huge variety of faïence available, most of it 19th or 20th-century work, including souvenir wares, clocks, wall plates and plaques, tea and dinner ware, mandolins and bagpipes, trinket boxes made in the shapes of miniature tables and chairs, tiny desks with pull-out drawers, menu holders, picture frames and tiles. Many of the finest pieces are naturally found for sale in France, but they tend to command higher prices there.

Faïence, by its nature, is very liable to chip or flake at the edges, so condition tends to be less important than with most other types of pottery.

▲ *These wares all show the bright painting typical of faïence. The price guides read from left to right.* ❺ ❺ ❻ ❻

▶ *This unmarked cat, decorated in the style of Desvres, is a 20th century piece.* ❻

QUIMPER EARTHENWARE

TIN-GLAZED EARTHENWARE, WITH ITS BRIGHT FINISH, HAS BEEN MADE AT FACTORIES NEAR QUIMPER IN BRITANNY FOR 300 YEARS. EVEN RELATIVELY RECENT PIECES ARE VALUABLE

Quimper (pronounced campair) is one of the major cities of Britanny and has been a centre of pottery production since the late 17th century. Quimper's first factory was established about 1695.

To most of today's collectors, the best known Quimper wares are decorated with paintings of Breton men and women who are dressed in traditional costume and carrying out everyday tasks, but that is just a tiny part of the factories' output. The early production included some fine decorative wares and figures which drew on influences from Rouen,

▼ *Rim chipping reduces the price of this Quimper plate from the 1930s.* ❺

QUIMPER WALL PLAQUE

Wall plates were a standby of the Quimper factories. This one shows a typical scene from Breton life. The man wears traditional costume and plays the bagpipes. The scrolled rococo rim is embell-ished with an inner border of *décor riche*.

Marseilles, and other famous French *faïenceries*. Apart from artistic pieces and figures, the factories also produced a huge amount of useful wares, particularly tableware.

Most are brightly painted with bold designs in vivid colours – red, yellow, blue and green set against a white or (a Quimper speciality) rich yellow background. The bagpipe, a favourite Breton instrument, features strongly as a motif, as does the cockerel. Simple floral borders are the norm. In contrast, ware was also produced showing scenes of everyday life in exquisite detail and pastel colours. The borders featured richly coloured leafy scrolls.

Premium prices are usually paid for early pieces, and for signed figures by known artists, but wares that were made from the late 19th century onwards are quite affordable. Pieces with detailed drawings and richly coloured or otherwise ornate borders will be more expensive, while the popularity of wares whose decoration has a distinctly Breton flavour makes them more collectable than those painted with other subjects. There is such a wide range of wares that collectors tend to specialize from the beginning.

▼ *This figure was made by a known artist, René Quillivic, in the 1930s.* ❼

ENGLISH MAJOLICA

THE BRIGHT COLOURS AND BOLD MOULDING OF MAJOLICA WARES MADE THEM A GREAT SUCCESS ON THEIR INTRODUCTION IN THE MID-19TH CENTURY, AND THEY ARE AGAIN POPULAR TODAY

I n 1836, Herbert Minton took over the Minton pottery in Stoke after the death of his father, Thomas Minton. Herbert was an innovator and he employed a Frenchman, Leon Arnoux, who developed a cane-coloured earthenware decorated with brightly coloured translucent lead glazes. Minton called the style 'majolica', after *maiolica*, a tin-glazed earthenware produced in Italy since the 13th century. Minton's majolica resembled the Italian work in its brilliant colours and bold moulding.

There were two styles of Minton majolica. One reproduced Italian wares in the neo-classical and rococo styles, while the other was based on more naturalistic modelling and colouring. The second type was more popular with the Victorians, not least because of the

▼ *This strawberry basket was produced in 1873 by George Jones.* **9**

---

*D*EALERS' TIPS

- **Majolica wares are easy to recognize and are rarely faked.**
- **Witty or naturalistic modelling is highly prized.**
- **You can get a list of the year cipher marks used by Minton from 1842 on. The standard Minton factory mark – an impressed MINTON and a printed globe with the factory name blazoned across it – also appears.**

humour that went into creating many of the pieces. Eccentric teapots were a staple of the range, along with relief-moulded and coloured serving dishes.

Majolica's popularity spread through Europe and the USA, and other companies were quick to exploit the new craze. In the 18th century, Josiah Wedgwood had created teapots and other wares relief-moulded and painted as cabbages, cauliflowers and the like, and his firm now produced them in majolica. Both Copeland and Royal Worcester began to produce good-quality majolica in the 1800s, while George Jones of Stoke made fine novelty wares from 1861 on.

Majolica has been one of the great antique success stories of recent times. You could not give it away in the 1950s and 1960s, but prices rose steeply after 1970, and are now at fairly high levels. Earlier pieces tend to be more keenly sought after.

▲ *The moulded fishes on this Wedgwood plate of c1875 suggest that it was intended for serving them.* ❼

▼ *This Minton dish of 1874 shows the basic earthenware colour in its handles.* ❼

SATSUMA POTTERY

THE JAPANESE PROVINCE OF SATSUMA GAVE ITS NAME TO A VARIETY OF WARES THAT WERE MADE ALL OVER THE COUNTRY AND EXPORTED ALL OVER THE WORLD IN THE LATTER HALF OF THE 19TH CENTURY

I n the second half of the 19th century, Japan, which had been a closed society for over 200 years, began to reopen its doors to overseas trade. Exhibitions in London and Paris, in particular, introduced Europeans to Japanese arts and crafts, whose exotic appeal soon found favour with collectors. One of the earliest products to be exported was a light, porous earthenware with a soft, creamy glaze that showed brown undertints and often had a very fine crackle.

The best pieces looked much like ivory, and were decorated with bright enamels and gilding, often in a different factory or workshop. This style became known in the West as Satsuma ware, though it was produced by large and small workshops all over the country. In Japan, however, the name Satsuma is applied only to pottery produced in the province of that name.

At first, pieces were decorated in a restrained manner typical of Japanese

▲ *This fine* **Koro** *shows commercial Satsuma ware at its best.* ❾

◀ *The understated decoration and simple shape of this piece show off the soft crackle glaze to good effect.* ❽

58

SATSUMA FIGURES

Geisha girls, samurai warriors, gods and immortals were all the subjects of Satsuma figurines exported to Europe around the turn of the century. This small, delicately potted figure with down-cast eyes is Kannon, goddess of mercy. The colour scheme, combining rich, deep blue, red and green with lavish gilding, is typical of Satsuma ware made at the time. Gilding does not always 'take' on the Satsuma glaze in the same way as enamel colours, and may be rubbed away in places, as it is on the goddess's headdress.

taste, with birds, flowers and landscapes but, from the 1880s on, Japanese potters produced wares specifically for European tastes; warriors, saints, geishas and dragons often covered much of the surface, obscuring the crackle glaze. Gilded floral patterns were another export item.

As the fad for all things Japanese grew at the end of the century, a wider and wider variety of wares were produced. The great boom in popularity of Satsuma ware inevitably led to a deterioration in standards. At the same time, however, and often in the same factory, there were decorators creating beautifully crafted objects for the home market and the foreign connoisseur, and these are widely collected today.

It is difficult to overestimate the popularity of Satsuma ware in the late 19th century. A contemporary English potter wrote that "the art of Japan has, in a remarkable manner, made for itself a home in the West. It has entered the drawing room and the library, the boudoir and even the nursery".

▼ *The fire dragon on this pot is particularly well painted.* ❽

59

EDWARDIAN ART POTTERY

ART POTTERS PUT ASIDE INDUSTRIAL METHODS AND USED TRADITIONAL TECHNIQUES TO PRODUCE DECORATIVE WARES

N ew techniques and advances in machine technology made mass production of pottery a reality in the 19th century. However, the great gains in output were won at the expense of individuality. A yearning for well-designed, hand-crafted pieces became widespread.

Henry Doulton, who had founded the famous Lambeth pottery in 1815, was one of the first to respond to the new ideas. Many talented artists and designers produced wares for him.

There were also several fine art potters based outside London. William Moorcroft worked in Burslem, Staffordshire, where he opened his own factory in 1913. Much of his work was sold

▲ *The three vases on the right were all made by Moorcroft, while the one on the left is by Della Robbia. The price guides read from left to right.* **7 8 8 7**

MAKERS' MARKS

Almost all art pottery was marked. All Moorcroft's work has his painted signature on the base (*left*). Before 1906, 'des.' was written below it. Della Robbia's boat mark (*right*) has the potter's initials above or below it.

through Liberty's of London. He was noted for his Florian Ware, wheel-thrown pots decorated with slip-trailed designs, a technique much the same as icing a cake. His designs favoured stylized flowers and foliage.

Harold Rathbone established the Della Robbia pottery in Cheshire, in 1894. He employed many young artists and encouraged them to experiment with ideas and designs. Della Robbia pottery is characterized by its bold colours. Some wares were decorated with sgraffito, where the design is scratched into the liquid glaze to reveal the darker clay below before refiring.

Another fine potter, William Howson Taylor, opened the Ruskin pottery near Birmingham, in 1898. His special talent was the creation of unique colour glazes. Just before his death, in 1935, he destroyed all his notes and equipment so the glazes could not be copied.

The art pottery tradition declined, but never died; today, there is a specific collectors' market for pre-war work, and particularly for wares that were made in the Edwardian period.

▲ *The Della Robbia factory favoured yellow and green wares. This vase was decorated by Annie Walker.* ❼

61

JUGENDSTIL POTTERY

WHILE ART NOUVEAU FLOURISHED IN WESTERN EUROPE, JUGENDSTIL WAS THE DOMINANT MOVEMENT IN THE CENTRE OF THE CONTINENT

The broadly similar new ideas in design which swept across Europe and the USA in the last 10 years of the 19th century and the first decade of the 20th were given different names in different languages. What was Art Nouveau in France and 'stile Liberty' in Italy was known as Jugendstil in the German-speaking heart of Europe, the Austro-Hungarian empire and the newly-united Germany itself.

It was in the field of pottery that much of the best and most characteristic Jugendstil work was carried out. The name, literally 'youth style', was taken from the title of an arts magazine.

Small firms in Bohemia, Hungary and the more obscure German provinces, rather than established potteries, were in the vanguard of the new movement. However, when it proved to be a commercial success, the large factories joined in, producing Jugendstil pottery and porcelain at every level of quality and price.

This aspect distinguishes Jugendstil work from the output of other European potteries. In Britain, France, Belgium, Holland, Scandinavia and Italy the proportion of Art Nouveau pieces to total output was small, and the new style was largely restricted to ornamental pieces. Jugendstil work, like Art Nouveau, has long, sinuous lines and shapes

▲ *'Melting' lip and handle distinguish this vase, one of a pair.* ❼

and decorations inspired by the natural world. A few later Jugendstil designers used abstract geometric decoration that looked ahead to Art Deco.

Jugendstil remained the dominant design form in Germany and Austria-Hungary until the outbreak of World War I.

Its ceramics vary enormously in type, quality and price. At the top end of the range are the individual creations by studio potters and famous artists. At the other end are the mass-produced pieces with which the German porcelain industry flooded the market. The best area for the collector is the middle ground of wares decorated with patterns inspired by Jugendstil, but not attributable to any big-name designer.

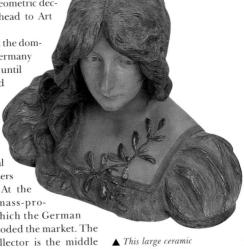

▲ *This large ceramic bust has the natural, flowing lines typical of Jugendstil pottery.* ❾

JUGENDSTIL DECORATION

Long-haired and diaphanously clad young women (*left, top and bottom*) were favourite motifs for decoration on Jugendstil pieces. At the other extreme, flamboyant geometric shapes, such as those incised on the vase (*left*) were also used. The general preference however was for natural, flowing shapes.

DUTCH GOUDA WARE

*THE ART NOUVEAU CERAMICS PRODUCED IN GOUDA AND OTHER
DUTCH TOWNS IN THE EARLY PART OF THIS CENTURY ARE
BECOMING POPULAR AFTER YEARS OF NEGLECT*

I n the last two decades of the 19th century, the style of decorative arts,
known as Art Nouveau in France and
Jugendstil in Austria and other German-speaking countries, swept through Europe. In
Holland, it had its greatest effect in the world
of ceramics.

At this time there was already a flourishing
pottery industry in Gouda, a picturesque town
in southern Holland. In the 1890s, these
Gouda factories began to make useful wares
colourfully painted in the Art Nouveau style.
Their popularity led to several new factories
being established in the town. Many of their
wares were exported, and Gouda eventually
became a generic term for any hand-painted
Dutch ceramics, porcelain included, in the Art
Nouveau style. The fashionable new style was
renowned for its high-quality glazes in matt

▲ *This sweetmeat plate
with a knob handle in
the middle, has a pattern
known as Rosario.* ❻

or a very high gloss. Literally thousands of different, hand-painted designs were used, though some, such as Corona and Rhodian, were used much more often than others.

Gouda ware continued to be popular after the heyday of Art Nouveau had passed in the rest of Europe. In the years between the wars, the patterns of decoration began to become more formalized, and the wares gradually took on a more Art Deco look.

The four main factories in Gouda itself were Zuid-Holland, Zenith, Ivora and Regina – their pieces are often very fully marked. Zuid-Holland wares generally carry a date code. A lot of high-quality Gouda ware was also made by factories in other Dutch towns. This generally bears the name of the town along with that of the factory or design.

Some foreign potteries have produced wares in the Gouda style, but these are easy to spot. Honiton potteries in Devon call their Gouda range 'Dutch Style', while Japanese lookalikes are invariably marked 'Made in Japan'.

Many collectors specialize in one factory, or even single designs. The Corona, Rhodian, Westland and Purdah patterns of the Zuid Holland factory all have their dedicated bands of enthusiasts.

▲ *The pattern painted on this candlestick is known as Mona and the piece bears the mark of an Arnhem factory.* ❻

*M*AKERS' MARKS

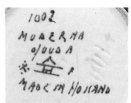

Gouda ware is often fully marked, usually by the painter. Ivora (*left*) included the pattern name and shape number. The little house (*right*) is a common Zuid-Holland mark.

ORNAMENTAL DANISH CHINA

THE HIGHLY DECORATIVE WARES PRODUCED BY THE ROYAL COPENHAGEN FACTORY AROUND THE TURN OF THE CENTURY HAVE A DISTINCTIVE LOOK MUCH APPRECIATED BY COLLECTORS

Though the Royal Copenhagen Factory is best known for its blue and white porcelain tableware, produced since the 18th century (*see page 38*), it also produced ornamental pieces. Many of these, and particularly the ones made at the height of the Art Nouveau period, from around 1890 to the outbreak of World War I in 1914, are very highly valued collectables today.

The factory was revitalized in the 1880s and a new artistic director, Arnold Krog, was appointed. New glazes and shapes were developed as well as a method for washing porcelain with all-over colour rather than painting small areas. Krog himself specialized in underglaze paintings in smoky blues and greys, and encouraged others to let Japanese influences into their work, particularly understated naturalistic designs. The results were very much in harmony with the Art Nouveau style. At the same time, the factory was producing

▲ *This finely modelled polar bear was made around 1900.* **7**

▼ *This vide poche is formed by the flowing hair of a mermaid.* **5**

a number of figures, particularly animals, which were made in porcelain, stoneware and earthenware. The porcelain pieces are graceful and naturalistic studies. Some were enamel-painted, while others had more experimental decoration. Moulded animals and people were also incorporated into the designs of bowls, dishes and *vides poches*, shallow dishes into which gentlemen emptied their trouser pockets before retiring.

The most common decorative pieces produced by the factory were vases, found in both earthenware and stoneware, though porcelain is more common. They were made in simple, elegant shapes and decorated with underglaze painting in muted pastel colours, mostly soft blues, pinks and greys. Flower studies were the most common subject matter.

The Royal Copenhagen factory mark of three wavy blue lines can be found on all genuine pieces. The factory's principal artists always signed their wares, and the right signature can add appreciably to a piece's value. Look out for the work of Arnold Krog, Gerard Henning, Berta Nathanielson, Jenny Meijer and Fanny Garde, among others.

Although reproductions and fakes by other factories are rare, many of the most popular wares have been in continuous production since they were introduced. A guide to picking out the earlier examples is that they lack the 'fraction codes' – giving the decorative style and number of the piece – which were painted on the bottom of each piece from 1894 on.

▲ *This porcelain vase in a misty blue glaze is signed by Jenny Meijer, an artist who worked for the factory just before World War I.* ❽

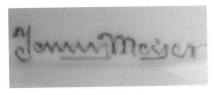

67

DOULTON FIGURINES

*STREET SELLERS, DANCERS AND DICKENS' CHARACTERS, VICTORIAN
MAIDENS AND REGENCY BELLES; ALL THESE AND MORE COME
ALIVE IN DOULTON'S RICHLY PAINTED SERIES OF MODELS*

T his century the Doulton factory, known previously as a leader in the art pottery movement, became famous for its collectable wares.

Foremost among these are the named and numbered figures and tableaux, known as the HN series, the first of which was issued in 1913. The first figure, *Darling*, modelled by Charles Vyse, was numbered HN1 for Harry Nixon, the factory's chief colourist at the time. Since then, all figures produced by Doulton have been given their own HN number. New figures are still being introduced – the HN numbers now top 3,000 – and old ones discontinued. Miniature versions were also produced, with the HN numbers prefixed by an M.

The factory often varied its output with different versions of the same figures. Sometimes the changes were just to small details of the modelling, but usually the colour schemes were changed as well. Between the wars, some figures could be ordered in special colourways to match the buyer's interior decor. Whenever a figure was changed it was issued with a new HN number.

▼ Butterfly, *first
made in 1925, was pro-
duced in five different
versions, all of which
were withdrawn in
1938.* 🝵

The original models were the work of a surprisingly small number of designers, of whom the most prolific was Leslie Harradine, who specialized in winsome ladies.

There are several reasons for the popularity of Doulton figurines. The main one is the quality of the modelling, remarkable in mass-produced pieces. Doulton have always employed the very best artists and designers. Another is the costumes of the models. Few figures were dressed in the fashions of the time they were made and often they were not strictly historically accurate. They made up for this however by giving a flavour of a more gracious time, even if it is one no student of costume would recognize. An exception to this is the work of Peggy Davies, who joined Doulton in 1939. Her models were always meticulously researched, and their costumes show great accuracy in their evocation of past times.

▲ Treasure Island *is the name of both the figure and the book he is reading. Peggy Davies modelled him in 1962.* **6**

▼ Repose *(HN2272) is one of Peggy Davies' more modern pieces, and was available from 1972 to 1979.* **6**

DOULTON SERIES WARE

THE ILLUSTRATED SERIES WARES MADE BY DOULTON SINCE THE TURN OF THE CENTURY ARE AS POPULAR TODAY AS WHEN THEY WERE FIRST ISSUED

Another popular collectable ware produced by Doulton was their series ware, ranges of refined earthenware or occasionally bone china pieces with several illustrations on a common theme. These were transfer-printed in outline then hand-coloured. The success of both this line and the figurines (*see page 68*) was due in part to John. Noke, a modeller and designer who worked at the Staffordshire factory.

Once Noke had grasped the commercial and artistic potential of the series idea, new ones were introduced annually – in some years as many as 20 appeared. The first series Noke pioneered was issued in 1902 and featured jousting knights – it was known as Eglington Tournament. The Shakespeare series followed in 1904 and in 1905 came Motoring, a humorous series. Noke himself did many of the illustrations, as well as commissioning other

▲ *This plate from a Shakespeare series features Anne Page, from* The Merry Wives of Windsor. ❺

◄ *John Nokes' signature appears on the illustration for this Dutch series biscuit barrel.* ❻

artists. It is estimated that by 1940 Doulton had issued over 130 series.

Perhaps the most popular of all Doulton's series is the Dickens series, which was originated by Noke in 1908; some of the original sketches for the series bear his signature as Art Director. At first the series was available in plates, bowls, tableware, candlesticks, trays and vases. In 1917 it was expanded to take in toilet and wash-stand sets, chamber pots, wall plaques, ashtrays, tobacco jars, biscuit barrels, soup tureens, tea caddies, jardinières and salad and fruit bowls. It was withdrawn in 1930 and replaced in 1932 by a new, more limited range in brighter colours. In the early 1950s, there was yet another new issue, with the items available limited mainly to tableware. The Dickens series was finally withdrawn in 1960.

The vast majority of Doulton pieces are very well-marked. A version of Doulton's lion and crown trademark has been stamped on all pieces since 1902. All earthenware pieces have a four-figure design number with a D prefix (*see page 13*); the few made in china have E, H, V or TC numbers. Current production, revived in the 1970s, is always china.

▼ *This jug carries a scene from Dickens, the favourite subject matter of designer John Nokes.* ❻

ᴅEALERS' TIPS

- **The price of series ware depends on rarity value.**
- **Items from the Gibson girls series, for example, are rare and will command high prices.**
- **Early Dickens is more collectable than the later pieces, and can be recognized by the more subdued colours used.**
- **Any pieces featuring golfers are very collectable as are items showing fishing scenes from the Isaac Walton series.**

ART DECO TABLEWARE

DECORATIVE CERAMICS FROM THE 1920S AND 1930S BRING A WELCOME BURST OF COLOUR AND ZEST INTO THE MODERN DINING ROOM, JUST AS THEY DID WHEN THEY WERE FIRST INTRODUCED

A rt Deco had no single founder; instead it had a variety of influences including cubism and African art. Vibrant and energetic, it was soon applied to almost everything – from architecture to jewellery. In the 1920s, the introduction of Art Deco tableware came as a breath of fresh air; the new designs were instantly popular, being both novel and inexpensive, and people jumped at the chance of an affordable way to adopt the latest fashions.

The most noticeable characteristic of the Art Deco style was the geometric patterns, used in both painted designs and shapes. It was Clarice Cliff who first saw the possibilities of applying Art Deco designs to everyday tableware. Her products were a world away from the traditional dinner services that were popular earlier in the century. While working at the Newport pottery of Wilkinsons, she produced an innovative range of tableware decorated with diamond shapes and semicircles painted in bold shades of blue, orange, yellow and black. Encouraged by

▲ *This Susie Cooper teapot is in the popular Kestrel shape.* ❹

▼ *Subtle leaf patterns decorate this Susie Cooper dish.* ❺

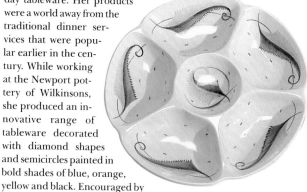

its success, Clarice Cliff produced range after range of new patterns, using stylized flowers, landscapes, houses and windmills, all in the bold and vibrant colours that became her trademark. One of the best-known of

these patterns was named 'Bizarre', while an all-time favourite was the 'Crocus' pattern. She was also renowned for her use of distinctive and unconventional shapes.

At about the same time, Susie Cooper was also devising radical new floral and geometric patterns at A.E. Gray & Co. Both potters made use of the improved production methods although they used hand-painting.

Thanks to their popularity, the output of Wilkinsons and Grays was dramatically boosted. Other factories followed suit and by the mid-1930s, major department stores were selling Art Deco ware produced by firms like Wedgwood, Worcester and Royal Doulton.

▲ *This Clarice Cliff dinner plate is from the Fantasque range, whereas the conical sugar shaker is decorated with the Crocus pattern.* ❼ ❻

MAKERS' MARKS

Virtually all Clarice Cliff and Susie Cooper ceramics are stamped. Clarice Cliff's work usually has her facsimile signature, together with the name of the pattern (*left*). Likewise, Susie Cooper's ware is usually marked on the back with her name (*right*).

ROYAL WINTON CHINTZ WARE

POTTERY DECORATED WITH AN ALL-OVER FLORAL PATTERN WAS FIRST MADE UNDER THE ROYAL WINTON NAME AS AN ATTRACTIVE BUT MORE TRADITIONAL ALTERNATIVE TO ART DECO

During the 1920s and 1930s the colourful and angular designs of Art Deco were all the rage. However, other more romanticized and rustic styles were also highly popular.

Grimwades Ltd. of Stoke-on-Trent recognized this trend. Under the name Royal Winton, they produced wares that had the flavour of a cottage garden.

Leonard Grimwade first had the idea of producing a transfer-printed, all-over floral pattern while watching his wife embroidering cushions, and in 1928 he introduced his first design, the Marguerite pattern: it was an overnight success. A less busy pattern, Delphinium Chintz, was introduced in 1931, and the name 'chintz ware' was soon used to describe all such all-over floral designs.

More than 50 floral patterns have been identified and named. Some patterns vary only in their colourways. For example, Hazel, with a black background, is otherwise identical to Welbeck (yellow background), Spring (white),

▲ *This preserve pot shows the Springtime pattern.* ❹

◀ *The Hazel pattern, with its black background, decorates this comport. This pattern is highly sought after.* ❺

◀ *Bedside sets are much sought after and are always highly priced. This one carries the Marguerite pattern, the first pattern produced by Grimwade.* ❼

and the rare Japan (vivid blue).

Other potteries, noting Grimwade's success, produced their own chintz ware, but Royal Winton remained the undoubted leader in the field, and still is today.

Most chintz ware was tableware, and sets, particularly bedside sets (a tray, toast rack, teapot, cup, cream jug and sugar basin), were a speciality. Some vases, wall pockets, and lamp bases were also produced, and since they are less common, they are more expensive.

Chipped or cracked pieces will be devalued, although they remain collectable, especially in a rare pattern. Avoid buying any wares which are defaced by tiny black specks in the glaze, or which show bad joins in the pattern.

MAKERS' MARKS

Marks on the base of chintz ware can help you to identify and date pieces. The pattern name appears in transfer-print, as does the backstamp of 'Royal Winton, Grimwades, England'; the different styles of lettering help determine the date. The backstamps date from (*top*) the early 1930s, (*bottom*) c1950, (*centre*) c1964.

NORITAKE CHINA

THE VARIED PRODUCTS OF THE NORITAKE FACTORY, MADE EXCLUSIVELY FOR EXPORT, REPRESENT JAPAN'S MAIN CONTRIBUTION TO 20TH CENTURY PORCELAIN

W hen Japan opened its doors to foreign trade in the 1850s, its people took to buying imports more readily than to making goods for export. Among the exporting companies set up to right the balance was Morimura-Kumi, founded in 1876 to export Japanese fancy goods to the USA.

▲ *The scene on this cup is quite common, making it possible to collect a full set.* ❹

In 1883, Morimura commissioned the first-ever Japanese porcelain coffee cups, made to a French design; after this they increasingly concentrated on the manufacture of ceramics. In 1904, Morimura set up Nippon Toki Kaisha to make porcelain for the US market. The main office was in Noritake, on the outskirts of Nagoya, and this name was adopted by the company abroad.

All Noritake porcelain was mass produced and sold at roughly the price of equivalent pieces in earthenware. A method of transfer-printing, employing wet paper, was used to keep prices down. It gave a finish much more like hand-painting than ordinary transfer-printing. The printed areas were touched up by hand, and whole areas were often hand-coloured. Even the smallest piece had some hand-painted area so it qualified for the title of 'Noritake hand-painted china', which was the way it was marketed in the USA. The inter-war years were very much a golden period

▲ *This mark shows the Komaru in red, and a pattern number.*

for Noritake, whose wares were sold throughout the world in retail stores and by mail-order catalogue. World War II put a stop to this, but the company restarted in occupied Japan. From the late 1940s, Noritake went from strength to strength, and became the largest manufacturer of chinaware in the world.

The great appeal of Noritake china lies in its diversity of shapes and styles and in the rich decorative effect of its bright enamel colours and lavish gilding.

All Noritake pieces are marked. More than 100 different backstamps have appeared over the years, but the most familiar is the Komaru, which looks like a daddy long-legs in a circle. The early Komaru was blue and printed alone. Later it was printed in blue, then green, then red, with the words 'Made in Japan' below the circle. If a piece looks like Noritake but has no mark, check the base for rubbed areas; some people erased the mark during World War II.

▲ This vase, one of a pair, shows Art Nouveau influences and was made around 1910. The price is for the pair. ❼

◀ These ash trays have strong Art Deco features and date from the 1930s. The price guide is per item. ❹

GLOSSARY

Art Deco A decorative style which became prevalent in the 1930s and which had hard, angular lines. The words 'Art Deco' derive from the 'Exposition Internationale des Arts Décoratifs et Industriels Modernes', held in Paris in 1925.

Art Nouveau The dominant European and American style of decorative arts from around 1890 to 1910. It took its inspiration from the curving linear shapes of flowers and leaves.

Biscuit (or **bisque**) Unglazed porcelain is known as biscuit, referring to its appearance, or bisque, which is the French term. It was more expensive than glazed ware because the absence of glazing and painting meant that any defects would be visible, so each item had to be perfect.

Bone china Stronger than hard-paste porcelain and easier to manufacture. Its ivory white appearance is created by adding bone ash to the ingredients for hard-paste porcelain.

Delftware The English name for the tin-glazed blue and white earthenware produced in various European centres throughout the 17th and 18th centuries. Named after the Dutch town of Delft, whence it was brought to England in the 1570s.

Earthenware Pottery which has not been fired to the point of vitrification and is therefore slightly porous after the first firing. It is made waterproof by the application of slip before the second firing, or a tin or clear glaze.

Faïence The French and German term for tin-glazed earthenware, known elsewhere as delftware.

Glaze Used on pottery and porcelain to give it a waterproof finish. Glazes may be transparent, opaque or coloured. The main ones are lead, tin and salt.

Hard-paste porcelain Made of china clay and china stone, the latter dispensing with the need for the 'frit' used in soft-paste porcelain. The strength and whiteness of the porcelain was improved still further by ageing the paste in store. The wares were then fired at very high temperatures.

Ironstone china A hard white earthenware, slightly transparent but very strong. Ironstone was first patented in 1813 by Charles Mason as a cheap alternative to porcelain.

Kaolin The Chinese name for pure china clay, a fine, white granite clay which gives hard-paste porcelain its strength and whiteness.

Limoges A town near the main source of kaolin in France and the centre of that country's porcelain production. As an antiques term it can refer either to French porcelain copying Sèvres originals, or in America it means any kind of ornate French-style porcelain.

Lustreware Pottery which has been decorated with a glaze to which metallic compounds have been added. During firing these compounds become iridescent, giving the pottery a metallic sheen.

Majolica An early type of tin-glazed earthenware which was originally Hispano-Moorish. The name is thought to come from 'Majorca' as the pottery was first imported to Italy from Spain via Majorca. In more recent times, the name 'majolica' has come to refer to enamelled stoneware with high-relief decoration made by Minton and others.

Meissen The most important porcelain factory in Europe and the first to make true porcelain in the Chinese manner. The town of Meissen is only a short distance from Dresden, and its porcelain was until recently called Dresden in England.

Overglaze decoration Pottery painted over the glaze. It allowed for the use of a much wider range of colours, as the paint was not subject to high kiln temperatures that would volatilize it. The technique was widely used in the 18th century.

Porcelain The art of making porcelain from a mixture of kaolin (china clay) and petuntse (china stone) was discovered in China some time between the 7th and 10th centuries but it was not until the 18th century that European manufacturers discovered the process. Porcelain can be fired to very high temperatures and is very hard despite its extreme thinness and translucency. There are three types: hard-paste or true porcelain, soft-paste and bone china.

Pottery Compared with porcelain, pottery is coarse textured, thick and opaque when held up to the light. Earthenware and non-porous stoneware are the two main types.

The term is also used to describe items hand-thrown by artist potters.

Sgraffito Decoration produced by scratching or incising the surface to reveal a contrasting colour beneath.

Slipware Earthenware pottery decorated with coloured slip (liquid clay) and then glazed. It was the main decorative technique in the 17th and mid-18th centuries, before the introduction of enamels.

Soft-paste porcelain First produced in Europe in 1738, it was made by mixing white clay with 'frit', a glassy substance that was a mixture of white sand, gypsum, soda, salt, alum and nitre. Lime and chalk were used to fuse the white clay and the frit, and the mixture was fired at a low temperature.

Stoneware Ordinary earthenware fired at a temperature high enough to partially vitrify the ingredients and make it impervious to liquids even when unglazed.

Transfer printing A way of decorating ceramic surfaces which is used for mass-produced articles, as it is quicker and cheaper than hand-painting. Early transfer prints were simply monochrome outlines, produced by inking an engraved copper plate, taking a print from it and pressing it on to a glazed surface.

Underglaze decoration Decorated before it has been glazed. One of the best-known types is underglaze blue, the ancient Chinese technique of applying cobalt blue pigment to white porcelain, much copied on European delftware and soft-paste porcelain.

INDEX